So I Will
Till the Ground

Books by Gregory Djanikian

So I Will
Till the Ground

poems by Gregory Djanikian

Carnegie Mellon University Press
Pittsburgh 2007

Acknowledgments

Grateful acknowledgment is made to the editors of the following journals in which some of these poems first appeared:

The American Poetry Review: "What I Can Tell You"; *Ararat*: "Diaspora," "In My Dream I Tell My Grandfather About the Voices," "Deportation Schedule," "Visiting Family"; *Boulevard*: "When I Saw My Grandfather Taking a Bath"; *Forgotten Genocides of the 20th Century* (anthology): "Geography Lesson," "History Test," "Armenian Primer"; *Free Lunch*: "Whenever I Had American Friends Over"; *The Georgia Review*: "The Aestheticians of Genocide," "The Soldiers," "How We Practiced Being American," "July 20, 1969"; *The Iowa Review*: "Suez War," "In the New Church"; *Nightsun*: "Children's Lullaby," "My Name Brings Me to a Notion of Splendor"; *Poetry*: "Kharpert, Turkey 1915," "Armenian Pastoral, 1915," "First Supper in the New Country," "A Brief History of Border Crossings," "Immigrant Picnic," "I Ask My Grandmother If We Can Make Lahmajoun," "Buying a Rug," "Mystery Farm Road"; *Washington Square*: "In the City of Languages"; *X Connect*: "The Armenian Question, 1915," "Covenant," "For the Sake of Argument," "How My Grandfather Escaped," "When I Was Very Young," The Electrolux Salesman Visits Our Apartment," "Oklahoma"

A group of these poems won the 2002 Friends of Literature Prize awarded by *Poetry* magazine.
"Immigrant Picnic" was reprinted in *The Best American Poems of 2000* and *The Poetry Daily Anthology of 366 Poems*. "The Soldiers" was reprinted in *180 More*, ed. Billy Collins.

Thanks to Julia Alvarez, Emily Hsu, Ron Offen, and Alysa Bennett for their very helpful suggestions and to the Corporation of Yaddo for two visits during which part of this book was written.

Several studies were consulted for some of these poems, but chief among them are Dickran Boyajian's *Armenia, A Case for the Forgotten Genocide*; Viscount Bryce's *The Treatment of Armenians Under the Ottoman Empire*; Leo Kuper's *Genocide*; Donald E. Miller and Lorna Touryan Miller's *Survivors: An Oral History of the Armenian Genocide*; Henry Morgenthau's *Ambassador Morgenthau's Story*; and Samantha Power's *"A Problem from Hell": America and the Age of Genocide*.

Book design: Michael Szczerban

The publication of this book is supported by a grant from the Pennsylvania Council on the Arts.

Library of Congress Control Number: 2006922934
ISBN-13: 978-0-88748-474-2
ISBN-10: 0-88748-474-3
ISBN-13: 978-0-88748-462-9 Pbk.
ISBN-10: 0-88748-462-X Pbk.

PENNSYLVANIA COUNCIL ON THE ARTS
40th Anniversary

Contents

Contents

III

For My Grandfather, Kevork Kayarian

*The struggle of man against power is the
struggle of memory against forgetting.*
—Milan Kundera

*Stories are for those late hours in the night
when you can't remember how you got from
where you were to where you are.*
—Tim O'Brien

I

The Aestheticians of Genocide

It's a problem of inflection really,
how we have to speak about it with some sense
of distance as though from a far hill
or a room with no windows.

The trick is to avoid excesses
of horror so as not to scorch the mind
and strike it dumb, though grief may yowl
in the dirt and the villages burn.

For instance, if we were to say
they brought the men to the square
and bound them to the posts and one
by one gouged out their eyes,
how many of us would turn
away in disgust, witnesses
only to our own revulsion?

And could we risk *throwing*
children half-alive into a well
until it was—already we feel uncomfortable
with darkness and water and the sheer
weight of suffering, must we add—
packed to the top?

It's a question of tact, after all,
how when we say *they had no hands or feet*
we mean to imply the butcher's knife as well,
the wrists tied down, the blade
seesawing through the bones.

Now, imagine a woman giving birth
by a river—the Euphrates let's say—
after her long deportation through the desert,
the soldiers around her laughing
and pointing their swords at her belly

as the baby comes *and then*—
must we say it?—*they are slicing her open,*
they are shoving her baby back in.

Admittedly, some facts stare back at us
with such severity, we must either
flinch or cry out. But isn't it the shape
of horror we're after, the poignancy
of our own trembling sensations,
not the horror itself, not the lash
of every gruesome detail
on our own skin?

For instance, the deserts of Der-El-Zor,
the starvation camps, the thousand hands
reaching for a piece of bread:
weren't those hands like the wings
of thin, bruised birds?

In Kharpert, everyone knew the boys
with good heads on their shoulders.

Along the Euphrates, some women
died in their own blood, and some,
holding their children close,
threw themselves into the river:

say the sun was too harsh and blinding,
say the river was beautiful once.

Geography Lesson

There is no country called Armenia.
—a 9th grade geography teacher, 1999

Where is the country, Armenia?
Is it on the map I carry
in my pocket, creased
a hundred times, a hundred
different boundaries coming and going?

Is it an island floating
in my imagination
at the edge of the ocean?

Is it like a stone in my heart
lodging deeper with each step?

Could I retrieve it, could I say
Yes, here it is like a trick coin
in the palm of my hand?

And if it disappeared as before
into the darker folds of history,
would I remember its shining
or say *gold like my grandfather's ring*
or *the speckles in my mother's eyes*?

Quickly now, before the world
rehews itself with a clatter of knives,
let me close my eyes, ride the wind
from the Caucasus down to any village:

Where are the fruit trees
rising in every courtyard,
children as spry as lambs
before the slaughter?

What is the shape of the country
within a country that no one remembers,
and where is the map of that sorrow?

History Test

The Armenian genocide is the "forgotten genocide,"
remembered mainly by Armenians.

—Leo Kuper, *Genocide*

Now, what happened in 1915?
There was a war, I remember, a conflagration,
the world was on fire, there were trenches of despair,
a no-man's-land in the heart of Europe.

And what happened in 1915?
It was dark, and there was smoke rising
like a plume on the horizon
where hardly anyone traveled
and the telegraph wires hummed in secret.

And what happened in 1915?
A disturbance somewhere east of us,
in the Turkish interior, clouds of dust
under the horses' hooves, soldiers
amassing in a clatter of steel.

No, what happened in 1915?
I remember the names of the vilayets,
Bitlis, Kharpert, Trabizond, Erzerum, places
which are even now difficult to imagine,
sounding ancestral, of another time.

And in 1915?
It began with the town crier
proclaiming the hour of deportation
in the village squares, it began
with the names of families—
Arslanian, Garbisian, Kayarian—every *ian*
tolling like a bell the sound of departure.
It began with caravans of children,
great-aunts, grandparents in carts, women
with a bag of household goods on their backs.

And in 1915?
It ended in the deserts at Der-El-Zor
after months of walking
with hardly any news of its ending.

Once more, in 1915?
There were long marches without rest,
many felled by exhaustion.
The men had been separated almost from the start,
led off to the neighboring groves.

No, in 1915?
They had been shot in the neighboring groves,
shot, axed, sliced, does it matter how?
Invisible like smoke, dust.

And in 1915?
The women and children bedraggled,
with nothing to eat but tendrils
of grass, seeds picked out of animal dung,
made to thirst even as they passed
puddles of rainwater, rivers
that followed them in whispers.

And in 1915?
There was a cataclysm in Europe,
a conflagration, who remembers
the dark, peripheral occurrence
in light of all that bedazzlement?

But in 1915?
A million dead and counting.

In 1915?
And no one to stop it, no one to say
This is the beginning of our century.

Kharpert, Turkey 1915

It is hailing in the village
where my grandfather was born.

It is thunderous against the roofs
and stucco walls of the houses.

It is like a rush of huge water
coming from all sides,

like a thousand angry voices
falling against the earth.

If all the windows shattered
who would hear it now?

If the ground trembled
under boot heels and hooves,

who would pay attention
or cry out against it?

This is a fury of stones
falling without regard.

Cup your ears, shield
your eyes if you have to.

By tomorrow, even the hardest fact
will have disappeared like vapor.

The Soldiers

Their cruelty towards the victims grew greater
as their physical sufferings grew more intense.

—Arnold Toynbee

They took him out to the pasture
and shot him, a bullet
to the back of the head,

and the death was instant
but it wasn't enough,
they weren't satisfied,

so they cut off his hands
for safekeeping,
they ripped out his beard

and threw it to the wind
like shed fur from an animal,
and they said they felt better now,

too bad they hadn't done it
sooner, when it counted,
though something else

was making them irritable,
his looking through them maybe
with the densest eyes,

so they took the eyes,
and then the ears too
as if he could hear their laughter,

and then they decided
why not take the face,
the whole of it,

and they did, in one piece,
and left him open
and tipped to the sky

so that his daughters,
finding him like that,
faceless, barely himself,

were almost unable
to weep or anoint with oil
or to say this is ours

until they had turned him over,
put him face down, the blood
draining into the dirt,

and the body, as if asleep
and unremarkable, looking
like all the others now.

Deportation Song

*The intent seems to have been the brutal
extermination of everyone in the caravan.*
—from *An Oral History of the Armenian Genocide*

This one was given a week to get ready,
this one, one day, or none at all, hurry up.

This one hired carts and mules,
took rugs, a set of heirloom linens,

and this one sewed her money in her hem,
or a shawl, or in the lining of a coat.

This one hid in the pantry bin
because he was too old to walk.

This one had the scarlet fever,
how would she ever last an hour?

This one carried his son on his back,
it was the only thing he could carry,

and this one dressed like a girl in a scarf
so no one would use the cudgel on him.

This one was already being led away,
two shots ringing out sometime after,

and this one, using a cane, might have come
from any village, any quarter.

This one was butchered
with farm hoe or hatchet to save on the bullets,

and this one was crying for water
like so many others left by the roadside.

This one, for months, had been walking
toward the heart of the desert,

every shred of her clothing torn away,
and this one already had arrived

though no one had seen her,
bone-thin, with nothing to carry.

Children's Lullaby

*About this time, Turkish or Kurdish women would come
and take children away. Realizing that there was nothing but
death facing us . . . my mother gave me to them. So these two
women held my hand and took me away.*
        —an Armenian child-survivor of a deportation, 1915

If you're walking for a long time,
you can't think about tomorrow.

If you're walking for a long time,
keep your eyes down and don't falter.

Wolves are growling in the mountains,
they will come if you're not wise.

Wolves are growling by the roadside,
and robbers prowling in the trees.

One eye open when you're sleeping,
the night has many arms that touch you.

One eye open when you're waking,
sometimes day itself can snatch you.

If you dream of grapes in the arbor,
you'll wake up with stones for eyes.

If you dream of rivers winding,
there'll be gravel where you lie.

And when your father falls behind,
don't cry, there's always someone else.

And when your mother falls behind,
don't cry, and then, there's no one else.

Never ask where you are going,
the wind might blow your ashes there.

Never ask where you are going,
the wind is blowing everywhere.

Armenian Pastoral, 1915

Memory is useless if none of us
remembers the same things.

—Bruce Murphy

If Anoush were holding her child
and watching the sheep
carted off like men to the slaughter

and Armenag in his dark vest and trousers
were hobbling barefoot in the village square
toward the pockmarked wall

and Ashod in his prison cell
were counting the sprigs of parsley
that must be rising in his garden now

if Araxi were razor-thin by the roadside
dreaming of a white mountain
turning red in the alpenglow

if Antranig refusing to walk
were shod like a horse
and tethered in his own pasture

and Azniv were a wet nurse now
to a battalion of mouths
her infant slit clean in the straw

how long would it have to go on then
beginning with *A* and spilling over
into all the alphabets

before *mother sister father child*
could wear the same faces in any language
be cut from the same tongue.

The Armenian Question, 1915

How much more killing would it have taken,
how many more bodies piled up like rugs
along the roadsides, how many photographs

. . . mute testimony . . .

how much more proof, how many eyewitness descriptions,
diaries, how many official dispatches of outrage
from attachés, provincial consuls, how many more cables
from Henry Morgenthau, U.S. ambassador to
Constantinople

> *. . . history of the human race contains no such
> horrible episode. . . . persecutions of the past seem
> almost insignificant . . .*

from Count Wolff-Metternich, German ambassador to Turkey

> *. . . the misery of the Armenians is indescribable
> and far greater than we have been told. . . . if we
> cannot act . . .*

how many more accounts by foreigners caught up
in the nightmare journey, nurses, doctors,
how many by Martin Niepage who could see
the starvation camps from his classroom,
the children emaciated, having forgotten
how to eat

> *Amid such surroundings, how are we . . . to decline
> and conjugate irrelevant words. . . . our educational work
> becomes a mockery of human sympathy . . .*

by relief workers in the eastern provinces,
by Europeans traveling on business
who could only watch from their windows,
hear the appeals for bread from their rooftops

> *. . . the most dreadful massacres. . . .*
> *everlasting infamy will be attached . . .*

how many stories in *The New York Times* of the exterminations,
more than the 145 already run—
> *atrocities . . . surpassing the savagery of Genghis Khan*
> *and Tamerlane. . . . even the most hardened heart*
> *must bleed . . .*

how many letters on the editorial pages by witnesses
who could scarcely endure their own words,
how many by Viscount Bryce himself

> *the story of these horrors must surely touch . . .*
> *no man in whom any pity lives can . . .*

how many speeches by the Archbishop of Canterbury

> *. . . not merely render impossible the continuance*
> *of the present horrors, we want to prevent their*
> *recurrence in years to come . . .*

lectures given by Armin Wegner, writer,
photographer, having taken more than 8,000 grisly pictures
and writing to Woodrow Wilson

> *Travelers passing along the road turned their eyes*
> *away in horror. . . . If you, Mr. President . . . championing*
> *oppressed nations . . . will not fail to perceive. . .*

how many more children bayoneted,
men carved up on the butcher's block,
how many women raped and left for the others

how many more before a word
might have been whispered in just right ear,
some small show of disapproval,
some signal to say
we don't intend for this to go on
something besides utter annihilation
to put an end to it?

Dark Wings

Now is the time to say
something for the animals

felled by gunshot and broadax
cluster bomb and bayonet

who have lain curled in their own blood
without succor or consolation

their flanks torn apart,
their fibulas shattered,

the muscles of their rippled
animal strengths untendoned,

horses in their heavy tranquility,
dogs snuffling the marshy grass

by river bank, by well-spring,
the sleek, undaunted cats, the goats

meandering by olive groves
without notion of bullet or

impending boom of artillery,
a hot sharp sting of pain

felt in the deepest folds
where nothing, neither claw, nor tooth,

nor talon, nor the brightest shoots
of light, has ever reached.

Covenant

*Tell the officials assigned this task that they must put
into execution our real intent, without being afraid of responsibility.*
     —Talaat Bey, Turkish Minister of the Interior, September 9, 1915

If in some afterlife you could meet up
with the slaughterers, the dispensers of injustice,
the torturers who have cut, broken,
punished the body to make it sing
its hideous ungodly music,

If you could see them again
beguiling a roomful of their disciples
while in some catacomb, others
are confessing the last of their sins,

If you could stand before them
bearing the authoritative
scrolls of accusation,

If you had the power to do unto them
without appeal or reprisal,

Would you let it happen then,
would you sign the decrees, seal
the letters of transportation
to parts unknown,

Would you say let us extinguish
and let us do it slowly,
without anesthetic or balm
in the name of the fathers and the sons
and all the severed holy alliances,

And would you be the one
to pick up the first knife
and begin to do the work it must do?

For the Sake of Argument

For a whole month corpses were observed floating down
the River Euphrates nearly every day, often in batches. . . .
—from the account of a German missionary

Say that nothing
happened in 1915

no massacres in Zeitoun
no Van or Kharpert

no wild dogs lapping
at the throats of the dead

say there were no eyewitnesses
no missionaries in the mountains of Kars

no death caravans
winding through the streets

say there were no consuls at the window
hearing the cries

say nothing occurred
none of it a matter of public record

no million dead or million more
scarred into silence

say nothing happened
no one heard

and say the hunger deserts
were empty of all the voices

and the rivers of thirst
were flowing like other rivers

without memory now
of any of it

How My Grandfather Escaped

It's not clear if he bribed an official,
or he knew someone, or he knew
no one, not the mayor, or the consul,
not the soldier who lifted a sword
above his head ready to strike, but he ducked,
or he played dead, or became invisible,
or his neighbor came to save him,
said *I know him, let no harm come*
and none came as he ran, as he rode a cart,
journeyed by foot to Aleppo
or Izmir, to Constantinople
where he took a ship, or he swam the Bosporus,
made a boat out of reeds,
made wings out of feathers and wax
he got out, he got out.

II

Diaspora

They appeared out of the deserts,
they straggled from the interior,

orphans, widows, a few lucky men
who were spared to continue,

they slipped out of Turkish households
under cover of night

young girls abducted for their good looks
children taken in as wards,

they came together to relief stations,
orphanages, refugee camps,

for a month, a year, staying as long
as it took to disperse like seeds,

scatter to all parts
from the eye of the storm

to Beirut, Nicosia, Piraeus, Marseilles,
even somewhere as impossible

as Switzerland, steeper
than Ararat, colder,

O Canada, oh say can you see
by the banks of the Charles, the San Joaquin,

ripples extending to Argentina
Kazakhstan, Australia, Greenland,

and, by chance, to Alexandria
where my grandfather arrived

and set up shop, and prospered,
marrying, having children,

bringing the rest of us
from a deeper exile into his life.

When I Was Very Young

Everyone was Armenian
and had an aunt named Lola
and an uncle with a gold tooth.

Everyone cooked like Araxi,
stuffing mussels with rice, hanging
cheesecloth full of yogurt
from the kitchen faucet.

Storytellers were everywhere
and they were all Armenian
and every story included a donkey
or a basket full of grain,
a village well, or an orchard of figs.

In each house, there was
Hagop or Adom or Aghavni,
and every room had an aroma
of rose water and clove,

and in every pew in church, Ymast
or Arshalouys could see the smoke
of the incense rising like prayer.

How many Armenians there were,
appearing as if by magic,
in the butcher shops, at the cinema,
merchants with spun-gold,
rug sellers with knots of silver.

Even the cemeteries
were filled with Armenians.

And the sea was Armenian too,
blue like the skies of Yerevan,
whispering in a language no one
but the sea could understand.

When I Saw My Grandfather Taking a Bath

He was a large slow fish
moving in the water,
the hair over all his body
rising and falling like tiny plants.

"Papaya," I asked by the tub,
"how many living things can you be?"

"Enough for a whole family," he said,
laughing through his teeth,
scrubbing the hard scales of his toes.

When he drenched his head,
he became the source of many waterfalls.
When he raised his knees, waves lapped at his sides.

"Papaya," I said, "your village
must have been by a river, and your parents
must have been fishes like you."

He stood up, water falling off him
in all directions while he soaped himself
the length of his body, the lather
catching on every small hair,
turning him all white.

"You've become a ghost," I said, "Papaya,
a ghost-fish like your mother and father."

"Like my mother and father," he said,
standing uneasily in the cold, trying to keep
his balance, and slippery as he was,
it took all his agility for him to sit back down,
sloshing in the water now,
half of him ghost, half not.

I took the washcloth from his hand.
I rinsed his ears and shoulders and arms
until all the white had gone
and he was himself again.

"Little fish," he said as he kissed my brow
and eased away into the water,
leaving on me the imprint of his lips,
pale crescent moons shining on a small river.

In the City of Languages

Alexandria, 1955

When we stepped out into the street,
Arabic swirled around us like smoke,
like a wind from the desert, it floated
down to us from the minarets,
it seeped into the folds of our clothing.

*

My mother would sometimes take me
to Hannaux's where she shopped for gloves
or a winter scarf, and all the sales ladies
spoke French and smelled of *Eau de Nuit*.

*

At Café Athineos, I would eat *loukoumades*
while my father joked with the Greek waiters,
and all around me there was silverware
clinking against the plates, like the sound
of gold teeth against coins.

*

I spoke too much or out of turn
on the school bus to Victoria College,
and for such sins a second grader will commit
I was caned behind the knees three times,
English rules, English justice, one, two, three.

*

One day, Daniella, our Italian seamstress,
told us how fearful she had been as a child
embarking to North Africa with her mother,

imagining the land wild and ferocious, the streets
of Alexandria full of prowling lions.

*

At the German School for Girls,
my grandmother had learned a song
about a beetle, and a father going off to war,
and she sang it, *Mein Kaferfliege*,
whenever I was ill or looking far away.

*

When I asked my grandfather
why there wasn't any Turkish to be heard,
"Never mind," he said, "let it be
as it is," and it seemed as if a wind
had come and swept it away
from every conversation.

*

Je ne like pas, a small girl was saying
in the restaurant, and it sounded right,
mixing it all up like that, everything
in a bowl, and no one way of serving it.

*

It was Armenian that we spoke
when we were together, entering it
like a house in the coldest weather,
shutting the doors behind us,
making small fires in every room.

In My Dream I Tell My Grandfather About the Voices

I heard it as I slept, Papaya,
a voice in my pillow, a woman's voice.
But I couldn't understand the words,
and I was quiet for a long time.

It was the wind, my grandfather said,
the whir of birdwing, rain on the leaves.

And there were voices in the garden, Papaya,
among the rosebushes and the red begonias.
I turned everywhere, but I saw flowers only
curling their heads in every direction.

It was petal speaking to petal, he said,
small bees vibrating to the hum of every grain.

Papaya, wherever I go, the earth
is speaking to me, as if there are voices
buried among the grasses, or falling
from branches, or hidden under the stones.

Pay them no mind, he said, *soon they will vanish
like a spider's filament, like wings in a green field.*

But why are they so uneasy, why
are they not asleep or in a resting place
or in the darkness which is like their voices?

*They are asleep, but their dreams are walking out
into the world like stories, like words in the wind.*

Who is the woman I heard in my pillow?
Who is she who comes each night, Papaya,
cradling my ear, pouring her voice into it?

No one you can see, a brief shadow on the floor,
moonlight splashing against the wall.

Then why are my ears always ablaze
or filled with the sound of a river
roiling against its banks?

Leaves falling on water.
Mica glistening up from a riverbed.

But was she your mother or sister,
was she your sweetheart with her arm in your arm,
walking with you to the river's edge?

It was summer, but the sky was a winter's sky,
and everything under it was a cloud of gray.

Can you not remember what she said,
walking with you along the apricot orchard?

There is no word that cannot be forgotten.

And can you not feel the evening breeze
brushing lightly like her hand against your cheek
before the darkness has fallen?

Nor any memory that cannot be undone.

Suez War

Alexandria, 1956

The sirens were wailing,
someone was shouting in the street,
and my father
was putting out the lights.

From a window, I watched straggler cars
heading home, their headlamps
painted blue and night becoming darker.

Everywhere, shades were drawn,
shutters closed and latched.

In the cold basement we sat
under blankets below the steel bracings
my father had welded for shelter.

Soon there was the sound of artillery
far away, maybe in Aboukir,
maybe shells aimed toward the canal
where already ships had been sunk.

"Hush, now," my mother whispered
cradling me in her arms,
the commotion of her heart
against my ear, and the radio's static
sounding like sharp bursts
of gunfire in the desert.

I imagined the apartment house shaking.
I imagined something like a large bird
curving perfectly toward our roof
and everyone suddenly taking flight.

"Hush, now," my mother said
in the flickering candlelight, the shadows
moving like dark wings along the wall
and the sound of guns in the distance
thundered in my blood
as my mother held me tight

as if I could disappear
like water through the fingers
or the flimsiest cloth,
or like a hand in the night
slipping away from another hand.

Deportation Schedule

After 1956 . . . and the tripartite attack on Egypt . . . British and French residents of Alexandria were summarily expelled from Egypt, as were many Jews.

—Andre Aciman, *False Papers*

And who will be next: Greeks, Armenians,
Italians, Jews, time running out,
time to set sail with only a suitcase,
no lump of cash, no jewelry smuggled
in the folds of a coat, no bars of anything,
no toys, no pets, no favorite books
to weigh you down, no margin for error,
time to crease the old life, put it away,
no lace pillowcases, or petit point,
leave them in the drawers with the silverware
as your grandmother did, and her mother, too,
no time for the rugs, Kashans, Yalamehs
in beautiful blues like the sea under summer,
give them away, no mosaics, no vases
even the smallest one under your arm,
no hesitations, no shrugs at the customs,
no saying no when you're told to declare,
no fumbling with keys in the dark of your pocket,
the *douanier* is sharp, he's got the knife,
he'll cut through the linings, break all the locks,
get to the truth if that's all he's after,
no goods to deliver, no secrets to own,
your life hanging open, and you're gone.

At American Customs

You take the smallest breath,
inhale a scent of something new,
like carpeting that's plush,
or the plastic in all the furniture.

Outside, it is cold November
when the threat of snow
which you have never seen
holds the clouds gray.

Everyone is wearing a hat.
Everyone is fumbling in purses and pockets.

You are holding your mother's hand,
you are carrying a small suitcase
of clothes and a few toy soldiers
from what might soon be your other life.

There is no one here you recognize.
There is no one to call you *cheri*
like Tante Chaké, or squeeze
your cheek like your Uncle Karekin.

Your mother is tired, your sister
wants to lie down, there are papers
to show, questions to answer,
it is such an easy country
to set foot on, so difficult to walk into.

Where will you live? How many friends
will you make? Who will sing you
the lullabies your grandfather has sung?

Your mother tightens her grip
as someone pats you on the head,
asks you how old you are,

and in your quietest voice you whisper *eight*
hoping you're old enough to pass.

At the far end of the room
above the glass doors that lead out
there is the large electric eye
that must see everything.

If you could confess, you might.
If you could declare, now is the time.

The doors are swinging open, closing,
the *whoosh* of great wings is in your ears
the sound of wings wrapping around your body.

You are standing by your mother,
holding her hand, transfixed.

Whatever anyone might tell you to do,
you would do it now, you would do it.

First Supper in the New Country

Uncle Hagop was grilling *kebab*
in the fireplace, sitting on a crate,
basting each morsel of lamb
with yogurt and oil.

"This is for your mother," he was saying,
as he drew the brush along a skewer,
"and this is in memory of your great-grandfather
who swims with the fishes."

There was hardly any furniture,
all our rugs had been left behind,
there were so many echoes.

Outside, it was Pennsylvania
heavy with snow, the sidewalks
had disappeared, streets had become
a mirage of dunes.

"Uncle Hagop," I said, "the place
is filling up with smoke." Our eyes
had begun tearing, we were opening windows,
flapping towels by the front door.

"Look at these beauties," he said, turning
the onions on their sides, singing
*O rise up my Armenian heart
above the jeweled Caucasus!*

There was nothing to do but shrug helplessly
as the neighbors passed by the door
looking in, amazed to see something
like a campfire in the middle of the city
and Uncle Hagop lifting up his glass
to the sheepherders of Yerevan
and the hardy grasses and grape vines
rooted deep in the rocky soil.

My grandmother was looking heavenward,
my sister was asking if we could return
to normal, we were all wiping our eyes,
waiting for sirens or the eviction notice

and Uncle Hagop was singing another chorus
about the heartland, forking the lamb
to its soft pink center, and bringing
platefuls of it like an offering
to the makeshift table

where we sat down, raising
a toast to the old life and new,
eating and saying as we ate
how everything had been done
to a turn, how really there was
no other way of doing it.

In the New Church

We were in church
but it wasn't our service.
We were confessing
but not in our language.

The priest had a beard,
but neither thick nor long enough
to veil the sorrows of the heart.

There were crosses on the altar
but none of them Armenian
flaring at the edges
like the fires of Van.

There were no censers
filled with myrrh
wafting our prayers
of intercession.

There were Stephen and Mark
but not Sahag or Mesrob.
There were Ann and Mary
but not Sandoukht or Sirvart.

Christ's body was in the bread
but no other body.
There was His blood in the wine
but no other blood.

There was the liturgy
bringing us to our feet,
the choristers singing hosannas
from the book of praise,

but there was another book
keeping us invisibly on our knees,
written in the names of our fathers
and for our other voices.

The Electrolux Salesman Visits Our Apartment

So he comes in, says he's got
what we need *hoses, couplings*

all you want
to make this a home

sits on a crate in the middle
of no furniture no rugs

just a film of dust on everything
like incense or fallout

and out come his bags and brushes
out come the filters and wands

he throws dirt on the floor, scatters coins
tosses confetti in all the corners

says *This is for the little woman*
and flicks the switch and the sudden vast

intake of air is something we've never heard
the floor humming like an electric grid

everything unsightly sucked up
as if it had never been, cobwebs on the wall

dust on the photographs of great-aunts and -uncles
peering out from a desert of silence

breakages and spills undone grains of salt
shattered glass in the deepest crevices

The power of technology! he shouts
above the whirlwind of cleansing

skimming over the floor from wall to wall
every shred every obstacle removed

surfaces so unblemished that for days after
we can brush our fingers along the baseboards, sills

over the faces of every photograph
without making the slightest mark.

Whenever I Had American Friends Over

there would be no speaking
in Armenian no wearing the old clothes
or referring to *the time when*
not even the names of foods
my mother had prepared survived
lahmajoun becoming "garlic pizza"
kuftas the Swedish meatballs
we never had everything rounded
into shape by the prevailing friendships
which were American and ok by me
like spaghetti in a can wall-to-wall
carpeting Joey pounding a ball in his glove
saying *whatta fruitcake* and me
trying to catch on to the implications
of Mary Ann whispering to Phil
in just *that* way what way? everything new
even my second self happy for all
that was left behind tarboushes
mourning shawls dark ephemeral
photographs of my great-uncles hanging
in the vestibules an ocean away wasn't it
why we had scattered to come wasn't it
to be near someone like Joey in a t-shirt
or Pete saying *holy moly* or *whaddya know*
or to watch Mary Ann in her kilt skirt
walking home sweeping mopiness away
and Bobby Lee making crazy faces
yelling *vavoom* and *outta kilter* and
the maple trees wagging their red tongues
and history something so recent it was
happening right now on the street
every word of it weightless
rising like exhalations into
the colorful branches

The Bad Boys of Junior High

If they could walk down the halls
without fear or containment
even if they had broken or stolen
and the punishments were about to come

If they could stand easily by the lockers
unfashionable insouciant never
outside any circle because they were
the periphery of all the circles

If they could lounge in the lavatories
stairwells as though they were places of refuge

If they weren't afraid of danger because
they *were* the danger if they weren't afraid
of change because they were the upheaval

If they didn't have to run
if they didn't need justice to get their due
razors in the dark of their pockets
knife blades in the boot

If they didn't begrudge themselves
their nerve who they were
didn't cower from the tumult
like bleaters at the end of the world

Then they were able to say
without malice or complaint to anyone
who would try to bring them down
*there is nothing you can do to us
that we haven't imagined already.*

How We Practiced Being American

It had to do with television, with radio,
listening to newscasts and sitcoms,
press briefings and Westerns,
it had to do with unrolling our *r*'s,
drawing out the vowels, as in "Mah fella Amurricuns"
whenever LBJ came on to tell us how we were,
had to do with *Cry-y-y*, and big girls didn't,
or mouthing "pardner" and "honeypie"
like Johnny Yuma in a rebel drawl.
We tried to soften our harsh gutturals,
the back-of-the-throat Armenian raspings,
it was all up front now, in the lips,
the way the tongue lounged tenderly
against the palate, touched it like a lover,
Marilyn Monroe at her sinewy best,
Elvis merging one luscious word into another.
*I'll have the fry-y*s my sister said
at the fast-food counter, lucky
to have gotten whatever she did.
Ah thankya, teach, I said to Mrs. Schaeffer
who couldn't have been less charmed,
failing me in spelling and social studies.
It had to do with the newness of it,
a history that was someone else's, beginning
only where the Atlantic lapped at the West.
"Four score . . . ," we recited, trying not to think
of our own dark past some eighty years ago
at the edge of an abyss, "Saratoga," we said,
"Oklahoma," making sure the *o*'s were long, long, long,
as long as it took "to form a more perfect union,"
something for all of us if we could just
say it right, find the key for the tongue,
a diphthong into the heart of it
where we could all be indivisible,
eliding easily one into another.

My Name Brings Me to a Notion of Splendor

No one could pronounce it
without mutilating spindling tearing
even my best friends would shrug halfway giving up
and always the long pause on the first day of class
after Dillon or Dinsemore or Dix
every face turning to me even though
my name was not yet called and mangled
in every probable way oh why wasn't I
Jenkins or *Jennings* something safer
and mannerly anything but this minefield
of letters set against each other sticking
in the mouth as if the fault were mine
as if no other name were as impenetrable
not Knoebbels or Steinbacher not Stoltzfus
or Schmidt how did they come to be
so inconspicuous who were they
playing kickball tracing maps of America
doing long division on the blackboard
as easily as if they were walking
across the street in their sleep no worries
no boundaries to trip them up no Mr. Bielfield
telling my mother *I'll straighten him out*
what was so crooked? even my past life
seemed now a dark labyrinth of passages
my grandfather standing on the wharf in Alexandria
waving goodbye and me on the great ship
waving back not knowing where the prow
would finally lodge on what rock what piece
of exquisitely verdant beach who knew
I would have to unravel the tangle
of circumstances that put me in a small
landlocked lumber town in Pennsylvania
face to face now with Joe Schunk and having
to explain the *D* was silent easy enough
to say once you got the hang of it but Joe didn't
and it was five or six fast blocks of losing him

down Hawthorne and across to Pine my heart
thumping and beads of sweat glistening
on my arms before I heard Louisa Richards
suddenly call out *DeeJay* to me from her porch
in a way that stopped me in my tracks
because nothing had ever sounded so good
and nothing came easier than to walk
up the stairs and sit down by her
and begin telling her who I was.

July 20, 1969

Where were you when Neil Armstrong
walked on the moon in everyone's
living room were you with Marie on the couch
as she lifted her blouse above her breasts
her parents profoundly out of town
and all you could whisper was *Oh geez*
while you fumbled with her skirt
and how could the two of you not listen
to Buzz Aldrin checking the list once twice
before the hatch was to swing open
and Marie asking wasn't it bad timing
and you bending down to her lips
saying *No this is great this is it*
toward the sweet surprise of contact
your head turned just enough to catch
Neil proclaiming "That's one small step for a man . . ."
before that giant plunge for everybody
and Marie guiding your fingers now
over belly and thigh *Oh criminy Neil*
her face deepening with intention
and everything in you trying to hold on
to all her brilliant surfaces wildly
against yours the room wobbling *Oh Marie*
and tilting toward Neil on the moon
so awkward in his outsized
boots oh everything so remarkable.

Out in Left Field Before the Citizenship Test

Only a couple of questions but which ones
as easy as pie but which pie

could I pull *Cumberland* out of the hat
or *Conestoga* or *bicameral*

so many late night tête-à-têtes
with *Baton Rouge* and *Pierre*

The Splinter, The Sultan of Swat, because
three strikes *babe* and you were out

like Grant in his tomb Washington at Mt. Vernon
more generals than you could shake a big stick at

I'd throw in Motors too
just for the ride no extra charge

no nerves now or clammy palms
no deportation blues or blues of any kind

because it was payday it was paydirt
it was pay-as-you-go and no looking back

quick now: Grover Cleveland or Lefty Grove
MM or Marvelous Marv

it was all or nothing it was the whole of it
in one package like insurance like annuities

something for down the road pie in the bluest sky
if only the tip of the tongue would work

if all the parts were oiled and frictionless
like a 707 sweeping miraculously out of the fog

no washouts now no out
of answers or out in the cold hoping

the immaculate ball
would drop in my glove

soft hands o gimme
please soft hands.

The Day My Grandfather Died

The clouds did not gather into a heavy gray,
nor did the flowers shut themselves up
under the easy midday sun.

The gardener knelt in the dirt
to continue pruning his roses,
the policeman sauntered up the block
without once blowing his whistle.

The trees were full-leafed and generous,
the river was flowing leisurely along its banks.

It was a day, neither cold nor dark,
when nothing unusual might happen,

a day as peaceful and orderly
as one might wish for one's life,
all the windows open, the doors left ajar.

III

A Brief History of Border Crossings

Inevitable that it should happen:
the bus I'm on pulls into
any sleepy town on the border
between here and the paradise just beyond,
and the old anxiety comes back—
how the rarest Chinese vase I've never seen
will suddenly bulge out of my luggage,
how the prescription in my pocket for lozenges
is actually a summons for interrogation.

Was it not so many years ago, in Alexandria,
that the borders around us were slowly
shutting down like huge metal grates?
And somehow we were getting out,
the *douanier* with a gold tooth
looking through all our luggage
and at the small boy who said nothing back,
repeated nothing he'd overheard
in parlor or bedroom alcove.

And at nineteen, when I swore
allegiance to the republic
for which it stands, I held
the Certificate as if it were a lost
occult text, the paper an unearthly green
like the color of play money.

So is it any wonder that even signs
such as "Entering Texas," or
"Welcome to New York," should shoot
a needle of paralysis up my spine,
like the heroin I've never carried,
certain it was there?

Now on the train to Tirana or Zagreb,
or in a burst of steam, to Paris—

City of Lights, city which must illuminate
all fakery and the shallowest deception—
the authorities are checking passports
(just the word *authorities*!
and the leather jackets bearing down)
and they are asking someone
two rows in back of me, *Are you* you?
and when my time comes,
how can I not give myself away?

"Relax," my wife says as we steer
toward the dark Canadian border,
"just let me do the talking," and I'm ready
to surrender to her American dazzle-
and-dare, though I've got my pile
of proof beside me—passport and license,
photo ID, pictures of my two kids
with our American dog, Dakota—
"Stay cool," my wife is reminding me,
"it's only Canada, you could be anyone,"

and I'm thinking of how any Tom
or Harry would handle it, the drive
to the checkpoint, the officer
sauntering up to the car
and looking me over, and nothing
about me betraying the 100 mangoes
tucked underneath the seat,
or the five cases of Mocha Supremo
in the lock-tight trunk, my face open
and friendly, without a flinch,
without the slightest doubt of who
I am, or am willing to become.

Oklahoma

They're having father-son breakfasts
all over Oklahoma today.

Maybe I'm making it up,
but I like thinking about that,
thinking about Oklahoma this morning,
saying the word *Oklahoma* and tasting eggs.

Maybe I like thinking of my son,
walking with him in Tulsa,
pointing out the oil rig on someone's lawn.

Here's Olson's Hardware,
and right next to it, Mae's Luncheonette,
just like anywhere except it's Oklahoma,
land of desert and sun and dust,
and corn too, I think.

My son says he's thirsty
so we get some Oklahoman soda-pop
made of sarsaparilla, with a touch of sumac,
and that's all right with him.

I love to hear him glub-glub it down,
tilting his face to the Oklahoman sky,
catching the last sip in the bottle.

We'd like to see a movie next,
something Oklahoman, with two steers in it,
maybe a pickup right out on the prairie,
and the stars just beginning to scintillate.

And doesn't it seem OK to use *scintillate*
in a poem about Oklahoma, or my son and me
in Oklahoma, because so many things are happening?

And should we wait for the movie to finish
or walk far out into that Oklahoman night
where the land falls off into darkness
and everything is listening to everything else.

Immigrant Picnic

It's the Fourth of July, the flags
are painting the town,
the plastic forks and knives
are laid out like a parade.

And I'm grilling, I've got my apron,
I've got potato salad, macaroni, relish,
I've got a hat shaped
like the state of Pennsylvania.

I ask my father what's his pleasure
and he says, "Hot dog, medium rare,"
and then, "Hamburger, sure,
what's the big difference,"
as if he's really asking.

I put on hamburgers *and* hot dogs,
slice up the sour pickles and Bermudas,
uncap the condiments. The paper napkins
are fluttering away like lost messages.

"You're running around," my mother says,
"like a chicken with its head loose."

"Ma," I say, "you mean *cut off*,
loose and *cut off* being as far apart
as, say, *son* and *daughter*."

She gives me a quizzical look as though
I've been caught in some impropriety.
"I love you and your sister just the same," she says,
"Sure," my grandmother pipes in,
"you're both our children, so why worry?"

That's not the point I begin telling them,
and I'm comparing words to fish now,

like the ones in the sea at Port Said,
or like birds among the date palms by the Nile,
unrepentantly elusive, wild.

"Sonia," my father says to my mother,
"what the hell is he talking about?"
"He's on a ball," my mother says.

"That's *roll*!" I say, throwing up my hands,
"as in hot dog, hamburger, dinner roll. . . ."

"And what about *roll out the barrels*?" my mother asks,
and my father claps his hands, "Why sure," he says,
"let's have some fun," and launches
into a polka, twirling my mother
around and around like the happiest top,

and my uncle is shaking his head, saying
"You could grow nuts listening to us,"

and I'm thinking of pistachios in the Sinai
burgeoning without end,
pecans in the South, the jumbled
flavor of them suddenly in my mouth,
wordless, confusing,
crowding out everything else.

Visiting Family

I'm in my mother's kitchen
with my dog, eating
pistachios and chickpeas
and having a drink, and my dog
is looking at me soulfully,
pricking her ears up at each clink of ice.

"Poor dog," my mother says, except
she says it in Armenian
which the dog doesn't understand
and can't give her that hangdog look
to prove her right.

"Ma," I say, "the dog is ok,
she's got more than she needs,
look at her eyes, all those fine teeth."

But my mother is opening
the refrigerator door, rummaging
through leftovers, trying to find
something that will satisfy.

"*Dolma*," she says, "always good
for the emptiness,
even if the belly is full."

We sit and chat about family,
great aunts and cousins in Cyprus,
nieces in New York, and further back,
great-grandparents in Adana or Diyarbekir,
the lucky ones riding the diasporal wave to everywhere,
the others dying in the Turkish deserts
or under the sword, but here we are.

Meanwhile the dog, wagging her tail,
has devoured the food in one gulp,

scoured the plate, left it
shining like a full moon.

"Poor dog," my mother says, petting
its head which is on her lap,
"look how we all want love."

And so we pass the late afternoon,
my mother talking about Beirut
or Cairo, about who has survived
with whom, rising now and then
to get more food—*feta*, *buregs*, *zeitouns*—
the dog pat-patting back and forth
without a care in the world
except for *what's next*.

"Ma," I say when she sits down,
"let me get *you* something," and of course
I know what she'll say, that there's nothing
to get, or what she really wants
is someone to undo the past
but it's like figs, isn't it,
how can you put them back
once they've been picked?

"I'll take a Bourbon and soda," she says,
shuffling the cards she's kept by her side
looking at me to see if I'll play,
the dog asleep by her feet,
the sun setting lazily behind her.

"Let justice prevail," she says,
dealing them out, and today, justice does,
giving her one winning hand after another,
all the wild aces, all the two-dollar pots.

She's so happy that she's dancing
around the table, kissing
her lucky fingers, and the dog
is jumping up and down now beside her
glad to be part of such a thing

and I'm emptying out my pockets,
throwing the few remaining dollars I have
over my head, riding one of those moments
you can't ever hold back on, or onto,
for however long it lasts
or however far it takes you.

Armenian Primer

The wound is there and does not go away.
It is part of the body.
   —from *An Oral History of the Armenian Genocide*

It is a language
with too much heartache in it
though the words for *heart* and *love*,

seerd and *ser*, sound almost the same.
Speak it, and a hundred ancestors
standing shyly under awnings

or behind lampposts
or in the shades of trees
will lean invisibly toward you.

Say *arev* and a warm sun
will fall on your shoulders
like your mother's hair.

Say *lucine* and the sliver
of moonlight in her eye
will find your eye.

If there are parched deserts
you have not seen, or rivers
that have not carried you away,

say *anabad* and *ked*
and the grains of sand and silt
will forever run in your blood.

In an ocean of strangers,
say *dzov* wherever you are,
and the sea will bear you home.

And if there is no home,
no hearth or village-well, no flourish
of apricots beside the garden wall

and only the unspeakable left,
begin again
with the first words,

hogh for the earth plowed under,
choor for the water
that has no history of thirst,

ot, *graag* for the air and fire
which consume
even the memory of burning.

Let there come orchards of longing
from each seed you root
into the riven fields.

Let all the words with an ache in them
burgeon like leaves
and rustle from every branch.

I Ask My Grandmother
If We Can Make Lahmajoun

Sure, she says, why not,
we buy the ground lamb from the market
we buy parsley, fresh tomatoes, garlic
we cut, press, dice, mix

make the yeasty dough
the night before, kneading it
until our knuckles feel the hardness
of riverbeds or rocks in the desert

we tell Tante Lola to come
with her rolling pins we tell
Zaven and Maroush, Hagop and Arpiné
to bring their baking sheets

we sprinkle the flour on the kitchen table
and it is snowing on Ararat
we sprinkle the flour and the memory
of winter is in our eyes

we roll the dough out
into small circles
pale moons over
every empty village

Kevork is standing on a chair
and singing
O my Armenian girl
my spirit longs to be nearer

Nevrig is warming the oven
and a dry desert breeze
is skimming over the rooftops
toward the sea

we are spreading the *lahma*
on the *ajoun* with our fingers
whispering into it the histories
of those who have none

we are baking them
under the heat of the sun
the dough crispening
so thin and delicate

you would swear
it is valuable parchment
we are taking out
and rolling up in our hands

and eating and tasting again
everything that has already
been written
into the body.

Buying a Rug

We're at a warehouse of rugs,
my wife and I, hundreds of rugs
piled up like flapjacks,
pass the syrup please.

Of course, I'm being flip,
but I'm after Armenian rugs,
and these are mostly Turkish,
I can feel the constraints
of history around my heart.

My wife loves the yellows and reds
which remind her of tanagers out West
where she's from, and the blues
are as translucent, she tells me,
as the petals of wild flax.

But I'm shaking my head *no*
to all of them, no to the Hereke,
no to the Seljuk, the Usak, the Beyshekir.

The Serbian owner is patient,
offering us coffee, explaining
about the different dyes, all natural,
how it takes three months to make a rug,
asking me if Turkish weavers
living in Moldova might be acceptable,
and I'm still demurring, I'm thinking
of my great uncles in a village
waiting for soldiers, or a thread of hope.

How about something Indian, he says,
or Chinese in a soft green,
and I feel more comfortable now,
the needle of my aesthetic distance
pointing to high, though if I were Tibetan

or Kashmiri, wouldn't I turn my back
and walk away, the weight of genealogy
and blood pressing against me?

The Fates must have been
rug makers once, snipping
and weaving into our lives
a record of all that we are
and are ruled by, the ties that bind,
the ties that keep us apart,
without alteration.

I'll take the Romanian kilim, I say,
even though I know the wool
comes from Turkish sheep,
and that's as a far as my hand
will extend today,
though it may be enough.

And the rug is beautiful, red-orange,
vibrant, perfectly made except for
the barely perceptible error, an extra
line near one corner put there
by design or accident,

like a thin scar maybe on the palm
of one's hand running along life and heart,
unobtrusive, making a difference.

What I Can Tell You

I found no trace of Armenians there.
All buildings in the Armenian quarter had been leveled.
—a survivor, returning to Kharpert after many years

I can tell you it was a village
fertile and full of grain,
that the moon grew full above it
before it darkened.

I can tell you that the figs
were abundant, their tiny seeds
were like small gems, hard
and round in the mouth.

I can tell you that the river in the evening
was like the dream of a woman
whose sleep lay undisturbed,
that the scents of mint and oleander
were the perfume of a hundred nights.

I can tell you that the women
halfway to the olive groves one morning
must have heard a chatter of birds
and the foot soldiers coming.

I can tell you that the men
deep in the fields of wheat
would lie down soon
and disappear into its many roots.

And I can tell you that the dream I have
is to walk back to this village
and stand in the square for a moment,
feeling the history of it on my skin,
a history of departures, vanishings.

And I can tell you I would like to hear
the wind moving again through the acacia leaves
and the plum trees in the courtyards,

and to hear a woman singing by an open window,
her voice like the sound of rain falling
and her hair as long and dark as the river.

Mystery Farm Road

You don't know how you've gotten here
what accidental turn on the road you took
while thinking hardly of anything

but here you are suddenly at a river
shaded by black willows on either bank,
the water dark and indecipherable,

and it is this river, you are sure,
that ran through the book you read one summer
as a boy in Alexandria

when the plains of Kansas were as far away
as you are now from your childhood.
And you feel a certain dizziness

as you see the railroad tracks running
along the river, and the small bridge
you've kept inside you all these years,

and the red barn on the other side
with its silver roof shining
like a vision of America.

How sure you are that the freight train
on its way west will soon pass through here
sounding its long plaintive whistle

or that the school bus you've always
wanted to ride through the waves of grain
will appear over the crest.

The book in your memory is riffling
its pages, whispering to you
though you can't remember the beginning or end,

only the farm, which is before you,
and a dog howling at the passing trains,
and a boy standing by a river,

and now another boy in Alexandria
on Rue Ahmed Shawky, reading a book
and mouthing the words *huckleberry* and *harvest*

that will cast a spell on him
for years, and that boy is you,
and the boy by the river

baring his calves under the black willows
is also you, look at him wading in, throwing
handfuls of water to the sky.

So I Will Till the Ground

So I will furrow the garden beds
with hook and spade
lay the edge of my hand
into the moistest soil

So I will plant artichoke and wild mint
because they are the splendors of any table
I will rejoice in carrot and radish
because they are the earth's own kind

So I will mulch the seedling tomato
that was my grandfather's preference
scatter caraway and clove
to retrieve the spices of his pleasure

So I will shepherd the turnips for my great aunt
who loved their soundness
I will induce the oleander to proliferate
among the four corners of my tending

So I will dig, perforate, hoe, scarify,
that out of these many wounds
there might come flower and fruit
to carry forth, to replenish.

Previous Titles in the Carnegie Mellon Poetry Series: 2001-2007

2001
The Deepest Part of the River, Mekeel McBride
The Origin of Green, T. Alan Broughton
Day Moon, Jon Anderson
Glacier Wine, Maura Stanton
Earthly, Michael McFee
Lovers in the Used World, Gillian Conoley
Sex Lives of the Poor and Obscure, David Schloss
Voyages in English, Dara Wier
Quarters, James Harms
Mastodon, 80% Complete, Jonathan Johnson
Ten Thousand Good Mornings, James Reiss
The World's Last Night, Margot Schilpp

2002
Among the Musk Ox People, Mary Ruefle
The Memphis Letters, Jay Meek
What it Wasn't, Laura Kasischke
The Finger Bone, Kevin Prufer
The Late World, Arthur Smith
Slow Risen Among the Smoke Trees, Elizabeth Kirschner
Keeping Time, Suzanne Cleary
Astronaut, Brian Henry

2003
Imitation of Life, Allison Joseph
A Place Made of Starlight, Peter Cooley
The Mastery Impulse, Ricardo Pau-Llosa
Except for One Obscene Brushstroke, Dzvinia Orlowsky
Taking Down the Angel, Jeff Friedman
Casino of the Sun, Jerry Williams
Trouble, Mary Baine Campbell
Lives of Water, John Hoppenthaler

2004
Freeways and Aqueducts, James Harms
Tristimania, Mary Ruefle
Prague Winter, Richard Katrovas

Venus Examines Her Breast, Maureen Seaton
Trains in Winter, Jay Meek
The Women Who Loved Elvis All Their Lives, Fleda Brown
The Chronic Liar Buys a Canary, Elizabeth Edwards
Various Orbits, Thom Ward

2005
Laws of My Nature, Margot Schilpp
Things I Can't Tell You, Michael Dennis Browne
Renovation, Jeffrey Thomson
Sleeping Woman, Herbert Scott
Blindsight, Carol Hamilton
Fallen from a Chariot, Kevin Prufer
Needlegrass, Dennis Sampson
Bent to the Earth, Blas Manuel De Luna

2006
Burn the Field, Amy Beeder
Dog Star Delicatessen: New and Selected Poems 1979-2006,
    Mekeel McBride
The Sadness of Others, Hayan Charara
A Grammar to Waking, Nancy Eimers
Shinemaster, Michael McFee
Eastern Mountain Time, Joyce Peseroff
Dragging the Lake, Robert Thomas

2007
So I Will Till the Ground, Gregory Djanikian
Trick Pear, Suzanne Cleary
Indeed I Was Pleased with the World, Mary Ruefle
The Situation, John Skoyles
One Season Behind, Sarah Rosenblatt
The Playhouse Near Dark, Elizabeth Holmes
Drift and Pulse, Kathleen Halme
Black Threads, Jeff Friedman
On the Vanishing of Large Creatures, Susan Hutton